BASEBALL
MATH AT THE BALLPARK

BY TOM ROBINSON

Published by The Child's World®
1980 Lookout Drive • Mankato, MN 56003-1705
800-599-READ • www.childsworld.com

Acknowledgments
The Child's World®: Mary Berendes, Publishing Director
The Design Lab: Design and production
Red Line Editorial: Editorial direction

Photographs ©: Richard Paul Kane/Shutterstock Images,
Cover, Title; Jeff Roberson/AP Images, 4; Shutterstock
Images, 6–7; Jason Tench/Shutterstock Images, 8–9;
Fred Jewell/AP Images, 10–11; Photo Works/Shutterstock
Images, 12; Bettmann/Corbis/AP Images, 15; Library
of Congress, 16; Eugene Parciasepe/Shutterstock
Images, 18–19; Tony Gutierrez/AP Images, 21; Kevork
Djansezian/AP Images, 23; Joe Mahoney/AP Images,
25; David Welker/Four Seam Images/AP Images, 27;
Eric Broder Van Dyke/Shutterstock Images, 28–29

ISBN 9781614734079
LCCN 2012946502

Printed in the United States of America
Mankato, MN
May, 2013
PA02182

ABOUT THE AUTHOR

Tom Robinson is the author of 33 books, including 25 about sports. The Susquehanna, Pennsylvania, native is an award-winning sportswriter and former newspaper sports editor.

TABLE OF CONTENTS

St. Louis Cardinals relief pitcher Marc Rzepczynski throws during a game against the Milwaukee Brewers on August 10, 2011.

MATH AT THE BALLPARK

It is Game 3 of the 2011 National League Championship Series. The St. Louis Cardinals lead the Milwaukee Brewers, 4–3. The winner of the game will move closer to the World Series.

Right-hander Lance Lynn pitched the seventh **inning**. He stays in to start the eighth for St. Louis. Lynn is tougher against right-handed hitters. He faces Milwaukee righty Ryan Braun, who is stronger against lefties. Lynn gets Braun, the league's Most Valuable Player, to ground out. Then Lynn is done.

Cardinals manager Tony La Russa has moves to make. La Russa turns to lefty Marc Rzepczynski to face powerful lefty Prince Fielder. Rzepczynski holds lefties to a .163 batting average. Fielder hits .306 against righties, but only .282 against lefties.

Rzepczynski gets the strikeout. It is time for another move. Jason Motte is much tougher against righties than Rzepczynski.

La Russa follows where the numbers lead him. Motte gets the strikeout, then three more outs in the ninth. The Cardinals are on their way to being World Series champion.

Batting average is one of the main **statistics** in baseball. Use your math skills as you take a look at baseball. You'll be surprised at how much they are needed!

THE BASICS

The Field

Atlanta Braves leadoff hitter Michael Bourn is on first base. He watches the pitcher closely. The pitcher throws toward home **plate**. Bourn takes off. He steals second base. Bourn must get there in a hurry. He has to make it before the catcher can receive the pitch and fire the ball to second base.

Much of the action in baseball takes place in the infield. From base to base, the distance is 90 feet. The pitcher's mound is in the middle of all the bases. It is 60 feet, 6 inches from home plate. Youth organizations, such as Little League Baseball, use bases 60 feet apart. The pitcher's mound is 46 feet from home plate.

90 FEET

60 FEET 6 INCHES

Batters begin at home plate. They try to get around the bases. If they make it to first, second, and third base, then back to home plate, they score.

The bases form a diamond. A diamond is a square that is turned 45˚. Imagine lines connecting home plate to each base, in order. The diamond that is created has four equal sides. There are four right (90˚) angles and two sets of parallel sides.

What are the perimeter and area of the diamond? Perimeter is the distance around a shape. To find the perimeter of a square, multiply the side length by four. Area is the space covered in a shape. Area is found by multiplying the length by the width.

Perimeter = length of one side x 4
90 x 4 = 360 feet
The perimeter is 360 feet.

Area = length x width
90 x 90 = 8,100 square feet
The area is 8,100 square feet.

Stadium Effect

Fenway Park in Boston is famous for the Green Monster. It is a 37-foot high wall from the left field line toward center field. It starts only 310 feet from home plate. More **home runs** are hit at Fenway Park because of this short distance. There are more doubles there than most parks because of the number of balls that bounce off the Green Monster.

Differences in baseball stadiums can change the game. Some stadiums favor pitchers. Some favor hitters. Rangers Ballpark in Arlington, Texas, and Coors Field in Denver, Colorado, yield the most runs. AT&T Park in San Francisco featured the lowest-scoring games in 2011.

ESPN found that 1.5 home runs were hit in Texas Rangers home games for every one on the road. The numbers for each team were expressed in a statistic called "Ballpark Home Run Effect." At Yankee Stadium, 1.267 homers were hit compared to each one in an away game.

The top home-run hitters in 2011 at their home parks are:

PLAYER	TEAM	HOME RUNS AT HOME	BALLPARK EFFECT
Prince Fielder	Milwaukee Brewers	24	1.062
Adrian Beltre	Texas Rangers	23	1.500
Mark Teixeira	New York Yankees	22	1.267
Curtis Granderson	New York Yankees	21	1.267
Jose Bautista	Toronto Blue Jays	20	1.186
Justin Upton	Arizona Diamondbacks	20	1.095

Find how many home runs a player would have hit in an average park. Divide the home runs at home by the ballpark effect. To make the math easier, round the ballpark effect to the tenths before dividing.

Fielder would be:
24 ÷ 1.1 = 21.8 home runs

Beltre would be:
23 ÷ 1.5 = 15.3 home runs

The Green Monster looms high in Boston's Fenway Park.

Playing the Game

Some baseball games seem like they will never end. The Chicago White Sox and Milwaukee Brewers went 25 innings on May 8–9, 1984. Some nine-inning games last more than four hours. The length of time needed for a game changes in baseball much more than other sports.

Extra pitches add time to a game. The St. Louis Cardinals defeated the Texas Rangers 6–2 in Game 7 of the 2011 World Series. The teams combined to use 11 pitchers to throw 284 pitches in a game that lasted 3 hours 17 minutes.

Texas' Matt Harrison threw 58.4 percent of his pitches for **strikes**. Percent means a number out of 100. To find the **percentage** of strikes, divide strikes (45) by total pitches (77). Then multiply the number by 100.

$$45 \div 77 = .584$$
$$.584 \times 100 = 58.4 \text{ percent}$$

The number of pitches and **strikes** for each pitcher in the game was:

PITCHER	TEAM	PITCHES	STRIKES
Matt Harrison	Texas Rangers	77	45
Scott Feldman	Texas Rangers	29	13
C. J. Wilson	Texas Rangers	16	10
Mike Adams	Texas Rangers	21	13
Mike Gonzalez	Texas Rangers	10	8
Alexi Ogando	Texas Rangers	6	3
Chris Carpenter	St. Louis Cardinals	91	53
Arthur Rhodes	St. Louis Cardinals	3	2
Octavio Dotel	St. Louis Cardinals	9	6
Lance Lynn	St. Louis Cardinals	11	8
Jason Motte	St. Louis Cardinals	11	7

A sample of games from May 31, 2012, and June 1, 2012, shows how the number of pitches can have an impact on the length of a game.

DATE	GAME	SCORE	PITCHES	TIME
May 31	Detroit at Boston	7–3	299	3:23
May 31	Houston at Colorado	5–11	278	2:59
May 31	Milwaukee at LA Dodgers	6–2	308	3:19
June 1	Oakland at Kansas City	0–2	253	2:24
June 1	LA Dodgers at Colorado	3–13	320	3:22
June 1	Chicago Cubs at San Francisco	3–4	255	2:39

Harold Baines (right) of the Chicago White Sox hit the home run that ended the 25-inning game against the Milwaukee Brewers in 1984.

Roy Halladay had a 2.35 earned-run average in 2011 to help the Philadelphia Phillies win 102 games.

Game of Numbers

A .300 or higher batting average, an earned-run average (ERA) under 3.00, or a team winning percentage of greater than .600 are some useful numbers in baseball. All are excellent.

Batting average shows how often a player gets on base with a hit. A batting average is hits divided by **at-bats**. It is shown as a three-digit number. A player with three hits in ten at-bats has a .300 average. A batting average of about .265 is in the middle of the pack of Major League Baseball (MLB) regulars.

Over a long season, teams are not separated by much. At the end of the 2011 season, only one of the 30 MLB teams had a winning percentage of greater than .600. Only two were below .400.

The Philadelphia Phillies in 2011 passed one magic number: 100 wins. They were 102–60 for a .630 winning percentage. That means they won 63.0 percent of their games. Only the Houston Astros and Minnesota Twins won fewer than 40 percent.

If a team has played 80 games and has a winning percentage of .550, how many games has it won? How many wins for a .450 winning percentage? How about .650?

$$80 \times .550 = 44 \text{ wins}$$
$$80 \times .450 = 36 \text{ wins}$$
$$80 \times .650 = 52 \text{ wins}$$

THE PLAYERS

Earned-run Average

Tom Seaver pitched from 1967 to 1986. Seaver did more than just lead the 1969 New York Mets to their first World Series title. He had an outstanding career with four teams. Seaver finished with an ERA of 2.86. Over his career, he gave up an average of 2.86 earned runs for each nine innings pitched.

Pitchers seldom pitch all nine innings. ERA measures how many earned runs the pitcher would allow over a typical nine innings. Earned runs are runs scored against a pitcher without the help of **errors**. A pitcher who gives up three earned runs in nine innings has an ERA of 3.00. A pitcher who gives up seven earned runs in 18 innings has an ERA of 3.50.

As the numbers get higher, the math can get tougher. A math **formula** can be created to make the process simpler. Multiply earned runs by nine and divide by innings pitched.

ERA = (number of earned runs x 9 innings) ÷ number of innings pitched

Seven runs in 18 innings could be solved as:
7 x 9 = 63
63 ÷ 18 = 3.50
The ERA is 3.50.

Atlanta Braves pitcher Anthony Varvaro allowed seven earned runs in 24 innings in 2011. What was his ERA? Teammate Randall Delgado allowed 11 earned runs in 35 innings. What was his ERA?

Varvaro's ERA is:
9 x 7 = 63
63 ÷ 24 = 2.63

Delgado's ERA is:
9 x 11 = 99
99 ÷ 35 = 2.83

Tom Seaver delivers a pitch for the New York Mets.

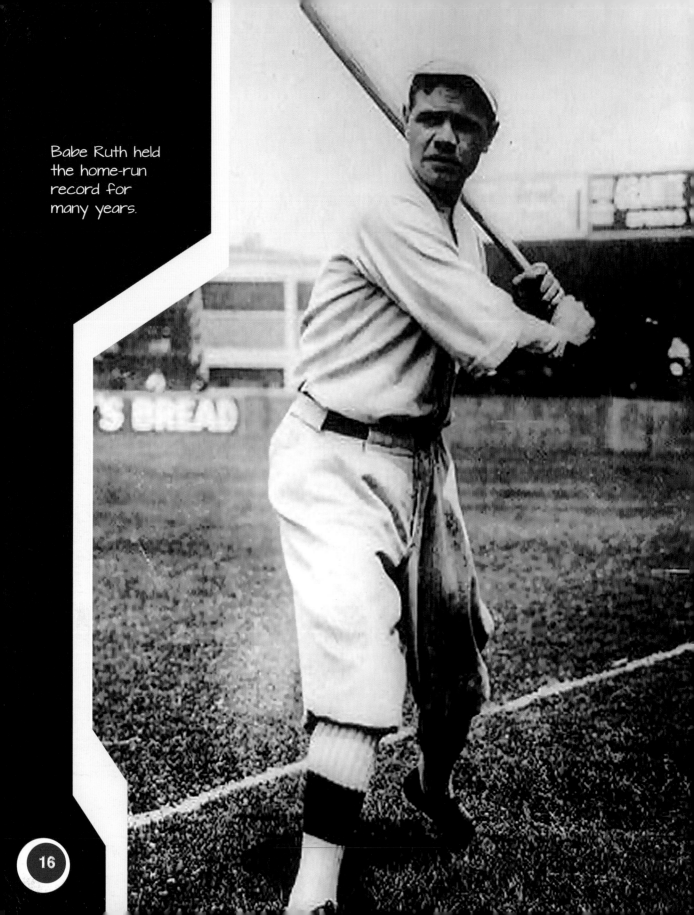

Babe Ruth held the home-run record for many years.

Career Paths

Hank Aaron and Babe Ruth ranked as the top two home-run hitters in MLB history until Barry Bonds passed them in 2007. Ruth played from 1914 to 1935. He spent 15 of 22 seasons with the New York Yankees. He retired with a record of 714 home runs.

Aaron played for the Braves and Brewers from 1954–1976. He piled up 755 home runs.

The double line graph tracks the season home-run totals for Aaron and Ruth. A double line graph tracks data over time for two items. Use the graph to answer the questions.

Between Aaron and Ruth, who had the highest single-season total? The highest point on the graph is Ruth's total of 60 at age 32.

How many seasons did Ruth play in which he hit more than Aaron's best of 47 home runs? Ruth had six seasons with at least 47 home runs.

How did Aaron hit more home runs than Ruth in his career? Aaron had better seasons at the beginning and end. Aaron hit more each year from ages 20 to 24. He again led at ages 39 and 40. He had two more seasons at age 41 and 42 after Ruth's career ended.

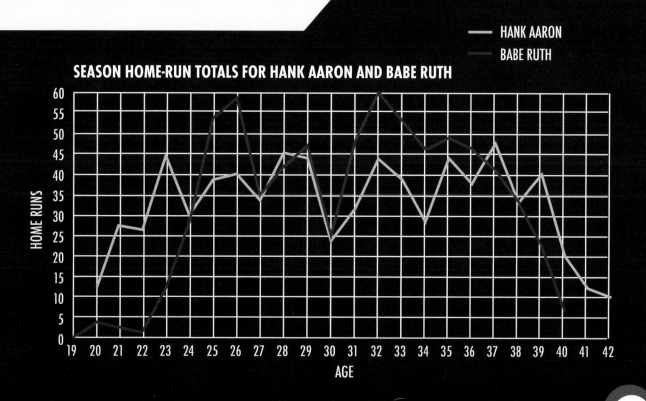

SEASON HOME-RUN TOTALS FOR HANK AARON AND BABE RUTH

—— HANK AARON
—— BABE RUTH

Magic Numbers

Babe Ruth and Roger Maris were a pair of New York Yankees sluggers. They were the only players to hit 60 homers in a season between 1900 and 1997. Ruth hit 60 in 1927. Maris hit 61 in 1961.

Beginning in 1998, the milestone was reached six times in four years. Sammy Sosa did it three times. Mark McGwire did it twice. Barry Bonds set the record of 73 homers in 2001.

Hitting 50 home runs in a season is still a lofty goal. Along with 200 hits and 20 wins by a pitcher, it represents a special season. There are also numbers that players climb toward during a career. Three of the most special are 3,000 hits, 500 homers, and 300 pitching wins.

A total of 28 players have recorded 3,000 hits through 2012. Derek Jeter of the New York Yankees reached 3,000 hits in 2011.

It has become harder for pitchers to win 300 games. Managers limit their innings and games more than in the past. Cy Young won 511 games in his career. He passed the 300-win mark in 1901. In the modern **era** (from 1901 to the present) 17 players have won 300 games. Randy Johnson reached 300 victories in 2009.

Derek Jeter waits for a pitch during a game at Yankee Stadium on August 7, 2003.

Twenty-five players have made the list of those with 500 homers. From 2004-2012, six players have reached that milestone: Ken Griffey Jr., Alex Rodriguez, Jim Thome, Manny Ramirez, Frank Thomas, and Gary Sheffield.

How many wins for how many seasons does it take to win 300 games in a career?

Top pitchers start about 33 of a team's 162 games. Each season it is likely that only a few pitchers in each league will reach 20 wins. A pitcher would need 15 seasons around the 20-win mark to reach 300 in a career.

15 (seasons) x 20 (wins per season) = 300 wins in a career
Even 15 wins per season are well above average for a starting pitcher in the 2010s.
A pitcher would need to average that level for 20 seasons.
20 (seasons) x 15 (wins per season) = 300 wins in a career

Slugging Percentages

Miguel Cabrera finished the 2011 season with two straight hits. A single and double by the Detroit Tigers player made his season batting average .344. It was the best in the American League.

Each hit has the same value in a batting average. Slugging percentage considers how many bases are gained by each hit. The formula for slugging percentage is:

Total bases are determined by counting each single as one total base, each double as two, each triple as three, and each home run as four. A .425 percentage is about average.

The Texas Rangers statistics from the 2011 American League Championship Series show some extreme slugging percentages.

total bases ÷ at-bats = a three-digit number slugging percentage

TEXAS RANGERS STATISTICS, 2011 AMERICAN LEAGUE CHAMPIONSHIP SERIES

PLAYER	AB (AT-BATS)	H (HITS)	2B (DOUBLES)	3B (TRIPLES)	HR (HOME RUNS)	RBI (RUNS BATTED IN)	TB (TOTAL BASES)	AVG. (BATTING AVERAGE)	SLUG (SLUGGING PERCENTAGE)
Michael Young	28	7	3	0	1	7	13	.250	.464
Adrian Beltre	27	6	3	0	0	2	9	.222	.333
Josh Hamilton	26	8	4	0	0	5	12	.308	.462
Elvis Andrus	25	6	0	0	0	1	6	.240	.240
Ian Kinsler	24	7	2	0	0	6	9	.292	.375
Mike Napoli	24	7	0	0	0	1	7	.292	.292
Nelson Cruz	22	8	2	0	6	13	28	.364	1.273
David Murphy	17	7	2	1	0	3	12	.412	.647

Elvis Andrus has all singles, so he has the same number of total bases as hits (6). His slugging percentage is the same as his batting average.
6 ÷ 25 = .240

Ian Kinsler has nine total bases. His slugging percentage is .375.
9 ÷ 24 = .375

Nelson Cruz hits the ball during a game between the Texas Rangers and the Minnesota Twins on July 25, 2011.

The Pitching Staff

Starting pitchers have two tasks. Starters need to last as long as possible. They try to hold the **opponent** down and put their team in position to win. **Relievers** take it from there. They combine to finish the game. Each team has both types of pitchers.

There are pitchers able to fill either role. But teams generally have a group of starting pitchers and a group of relief pitchers. There are usually five starting pitchers on a team. They take turns starting games. This is called a starting rotation.

Here is a look at the number of innings pitched by the starters and relievers of six teams in the first 54 games, or one-third, of the 2012 season:

TEAM	INNINGS BY STARTERS	INNINGS BY RELIEVERS	PERCENT BY STARTERS
Chicago White Sox	334	153 2/3	68.5
Chicago Cubs	316 2/3	158	66.7
Baltimore Orioles	319	182	63.7
Colorado Rockies	291	185	61.1
Minnesota Twins	284 2/3	187 1/3	60.3

To find the percentage pitched by starters, first add the innings pitched by starters to the innings pitched by relievers to get the total innings pitched. For the Baltimore Orioles, that would be:

Minnesota's starters lasted the least total time. They had by far the worst **performance**. Starting pitchers usually last longer if they are pitching well.

319 (innings by starters) + 182 (innings by relievers) = 501 total innings
319 (innings by starters) ÷ 501 (total innings played) = 0.637
0.637 x 100 = 63.7 percent

New York Mets pitcher John Maine (left) and third baseman David Wright wait for a pitching change during a game against the Los Angeles Dodgers on June 12, 2007.

Innings by Relievers

Innings by Starters

39.7%

60.3%

Circle graphs can show parts of a whole. The graph shows the breakdown of pitching staff for Minnesota.

The Batting Order

Managers not only choose the starting players. They decide the order in which players will bat. This is part of the **lineup card** turned in before a game.

Here is a fictional lineup of players with a set of statistics after ten games.

NAME	POSITION	AB (AT-BATS)	H (HITS)	2B (DOUBLE)	3B (TRIPLE)	HR (HOME RUNS)	AVG. (BATTING AVERAGE)	SLUG (SLUGGING PERCENTAGE)	OBP (ON-BASE PERCENTAGE)	SAC (SACRIFICES)
Smith	C	35	12	5	0	1	.343	.571	.425	1
Jones	1B	40	8	2	0	3	.200	.475	.238	0
Lopez	2B	42	15	2	1	0	.357	.452	.400	2
Washington	SS	40	11	1	1	0	.275	.350	.326	3
Johnson	3B	41	12	5	2	2	.293	.659	.356	0
Garcia	LF	36	10	0	0	4	.278	.611	.409	1
Chen	CF	40	13	2	1	0	.325	.425	.386	0
Reilly	RF	38	9	3	0	3	.237	.553	.310	0
Williams	DH	40	14	2	2	2	.350	.650	.435	0

The manager decided that he wanted the batter with the best on-base percentage (OBP) first. He would use the one with the most **sacrifices** second. The player with the best slugging percentage would bat third. He wanted the home-run leader fourth. Then, the best remaining slugging percentage fifth. Once those were filled, he planned to place the last four players in order of batting averages.

OBP is another way to judge hitters. It gives credit for getting on base in ways other than hits. That includes walks and being hit by pitches. The OBP is:

times reaching base ÷ total plate appearances

Total plate appearances is the number of times a hitter comes up to bat.

The highest OBP belongs to Williams. He will bat first. Washington has the most sacrifices. He is second. Johnson has the best slugging percentage. He is third. Garcia has the most home runs. He is fourth. Smith has the best slugging percentage of those left. He is next. The four remaining players are put in order of batting average. The order is Lopez, Chen, Reilly, and Jones. The batting order is: Williams, Washington, Johnson, Garcia, Smith, Lopez, Chen, Reilly, and Jones.

Colorado Rockies coach Tom Runnells updates the lineup card during a game on August 17, 2011.

Through the Years

MLB switched from a 154-game schedule to a 162-game schedule for the 1962 season. The 1972, 1981, 1994, and 1995 seasons were shortened. Contract **disputes** between players and owners led to games being called off. The other 46 seasons between 1962 and 2011 went the full 162 games. The St. Louis Cardinals won five titles during that time. The team also had some down years.

Average wins per decade shows the team's overall success during that time frame. From 1962 to 1969, the Cardinals won 84, 93, 93, 80, 83, 101, 97, and 87 games. Find the average win total in that span.

The win totals added up to 718. To find an average, divide the total from the number of items.

718 (total) ÷ 8 (seasons) = 89.8 games
The Cardinals won an average of 89.8 games each season.

The Cardinals won 725 games in 9 full seasons from 1970 to 1979.
725 ÷ 9 = 81 games
The Cardinals won an average of 81 games each season.

The Cardinals averaged 85.1 wins in the 162-game seasons of the 1980s and 80.4 in the 162-game seasons of the 1990s. The 2000s featured 913 wins in 10 seasons for an average of 91.3. The first two seasons of the 2010s were 86 and 90 wins for an average of 88.

AVERAGE WINS IN A SEASON BY ST. LOUIS CARDINALS

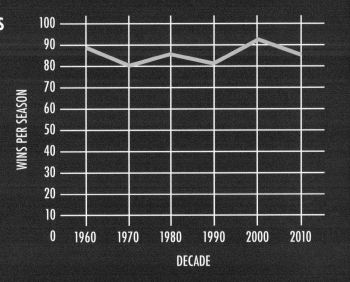

According to the graph, which decades saw a decrease in yearly wins by the Cardinals?

The line graph goes down from the 1960s to 1970s, from the 1980s to 1990s, and the 2000s to 2010s. That means wins decreased during those times.

St. Louis Cardinals players wait for the start of a game in 2012.

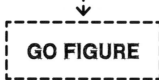

GO FIGURE

1. A player has 10 hits in 34 at-bats, has walked five times, and hit a sacrifice fly. In all, he has reached base 15 times in 40 plate appearances.

   A. What is his batting average?
   B. What is his on-base percentage?

2. After working 20 innings, a pitcher has allowed 7 earned runs. What is the pitcher's ERA?

3. A team has 705 wins in 8 seasons. How many average wins does the team have for each season?

Answer Key

1A. 10 (hits) ÷ 34 (at-bats) = **.294 batting average**

1B. 15 (times at base) ÷ 40 (plate appearances) = **.375 on-base** percentage

2. 7 (earned runs) x 9 = 63
   63 ÷ 20 = **3.15 ERA**

3. 705 (total wins) ÷ 8 (seasons)= **88 wins per season**

The San Francisco Giants play against the Oakland Athletics on May 23, 2010.

at-bat (AT-BAT): An at-bat is a player's turn trying to get a hit. A player with three hits in ten at-bats has a .300 average.

disputes (diss-PYOOTS): Disputes are disagreements about something, such as the terms of contracts. Contract disputes between players and owners have led to some games being called off.

era (IHR-uh): An era is a period of time in history. The modern era of baseball is from 1901 to the present.

errors (ER-urz): Errors are mistakes made by a fielder who allows a batter to reach base, or a runner to advance an extra base, or allows an at bat to continue after the batter should have been put out. Earned runs are runs scored against a pitcher without the help of errors.

formula (FOR-myuh-luh): A formula is a rule in science or math that is written with symbols and numbers. A formula is used to find a baseball statistic.

inning (IN-ing): An inning is a part of a baseball game in which each team gets a turn at bat. A 1984 game between the Chicago White Sox and Milwaukee Brewers went 25 innings.

percentage (pur-SEN-tij): A percentage is a number out of a hundred. A .425 slugging percentage is about average.

relievers (ri-LEEV-uhrz): Relievers are pitchers who take over for the starting pitchers. Relievers combine to finish the game.

sacrifices (SAK-ruh-fahys-iz): Sacrifices are plays that allow a runner to advance to a base, but the hitter is out. Sacrifices count toward total plate appearances..

statistics (stuh-TISS-tiks): Statistics are facts or pieces of information expressed in numbers or percentages. Batting average is one of the main statistics in baseball.

strikes (STRIKES): Strikes are balls pitched over the plate between the batter's chest and knees, or any pitch that is swung at and missed. Matt Harrison threw 58.4 percent of his pitches for strikes.

LEARN MORE

Books

Bertoletti, John C. *How Baseball Managers Use Math*. New York: Chelsea Clubhouse, 2010.

Jennison, Christopher. *Baseball Math: Grandslam Activities and Projects for Grades 4–8*. Tucson, AZ: Good Year Books, 2005.

Mahaney, Ian F. *The Math of Baseball*. New York: Powerkids Press, 2012.

Web Sites

Visit our Web site for links about baseball math:
childsworld.com/links

Note to Parents, Teachers, and Librarians: We routinely verify our Web links to make sure they are safe and active sites. So encourage your readers to check them out!

INDEX